The

OUTRAGEOUS
GOLF QUOTES
Ever

John McGran

**Andrews McMeel
Publishing**

Kansas City

02 03 04 05 BIN 10 9 8 7 6 5 4 3 2

ISBN: 0-7407-1909-2

Library of Congress Catalog Card Number: 2001086876

Book design by Holly Camerlinck
Illustrations by Kevin Brimmer

To my loving and supportive family: wife Barbara, son Jonathan, and daughter Caelyn Rose.

Contents

Introduction: *Fore-word*!

American humorist Mark Twain once termed the game of golf "a good walk spoiled." Since then it's been called a lot worse by the millions of fans frustrated in their attempts to master the process of using a stick to drive a little dimpled ball into a tiny hole in the ground.

But the game of golf has also been praised and lauded as everything from a religion to a philosophy of life. Heck, it just might be the most quotable pastime in history.

As a matter of course, we've collected a few hundred of the more printable ponderings from a small army of famous players, well-known sportswriters, and everyday duffers. So it's time to tee up and take a worthwhile walk through golfing history through the words of wisdom and wit uttered by such legends of the game as Bobby Jones, Sam Snead, Ben Hogan, Arnold Palmer, Jack Nicklaus, Lee Trevino, Tiger Woods, and many, many more. It's the par-fect way to spend that rainy day when you're not hitting the links.

Fore!

Golf Is . . .

"Golf is a game whose aim is to hit a very small ball into an even smaller hole, with weapons singularly ill-suited for the purpose."

—British Prime Minister Winston Churchill

◆

"Golf is so popular simply because it is the best game in the world at which to be bad."

—English writer A. A. Milne

◆

"Golf is the most fun you can have without taking your clothes off."

—Chi Chi Rodriguez

"Golf is a wonderful exercise. You can stand on your feet for hours, watching somebody else putt."

—American humorist Will Rogers

◆

"Golf is not a funeral, although both can be very sad affairs."

—British columnist Bernard Darwin

◆

"Golf is not a game of good shots. It's a game of bad shots."

—Ben Hogan

"Golf is essentially an exercise in masochism conducted out of doors."

—American writer Paul O'Neil

"Golf is a plague invented by the Calvinistic
Scots as a punishment for man's sins.
As General Eisenhower discovered, it is easier
to end the Cold War or stamp out poverty
than to master this devilish pastime."

—American writer James Reston

◆

"Golf is, in part, a game; but only in part.
It is also part of a religion, a fervor, a vice,
a mirage, a frenzy, a fear, an abscess, a joy,
a thrill, a pest, a disease, an uplift, a brooding
melancholy, a dream of yesterday, a
disappointing today, and a hope for tomorrow."

—Sportswriter Grantland Rice

"Golf is war. And like all wars, if you're not looking to win you probably shouldn't show up."

—*Army Captain Bruce Warren Ollstein*

◆

"Golf is a day spent in a round of strenuous idleness."

—*British poet William Wordsworth*

◆

"Golf is an awkward set of bodily contortions designed to produce a graceful result."

—*Tommy Armour*

"Golf is like a love affair. If you don't take it too seriously, it's no fun; if you do take it seriously, it breaks your heart."

—American actor Arnold Daly

◆

"Golf is not a game of great shots. It's a game of the most accurate misses. The people who win make the smallest mistakes."

—Gene Littler

◆

"Golf is a compromise between what your ego wants you to do, what experience tells you to do, and what your nerves let you do."

—Bruce Crampton

"Golf is like a razor. You get just so sharp
and then it begins to dull a little more
the more you use it."

—Doug Sanders

◆

"Golf is like a chain. You always have to
work on the weakest links."

—George Archer

◆

"Golf is neither a microcosm of nor
a metaphor for life. It is a sport, a bloodless
sport, if you don't count ulcers."

—Author Dick Schaap

"Golf is an ideal diversion, but a ruinous disease."

_FORBES *magazine founder B. C. Forbes*

◆

"Golf is deceptively simple and
endlessly complicated."

_*Arnold Palmer*

◆

"Golf is a non-violent game played
violently from within."

_*Golf guru Bob Toski*

"Golf is much more fun than walking naked in a strange place, but not much."

—Comedian Buddy Hackett

◆

"Golf is the Esperanto of sport. All over the world, golfers talk the same language—much of it nonsense and much unprintable—endure the same frustrations, discover the same infallible secrets of putting, share the same illusory joys."

—Golf commentator Henry Longhurst

"Golf . . . a young man's vice and
an old man's penance."

—Humorist Irvin S. Cobb

◆

"Golf is a funny game. It's done much for health
and at the same time has ruined people by
robbing them of their peace of mind. Look at me,
I'm the healthiest idiot in the world."

—Comedian Bob Hope

"Golf is a lot like sex. It's something you can enjoy all your life. And if you remain an amateur, you get to pick your own playing partners."

—*Inaugural U.S. Walker Cup team member Jess Sweetser*

◆

"Golf is an expensive way of playing marbles."

—*Writer G. K. Chesterton*

◆

"Golf is a diabolical game. It's easy to make fun of something that's so bizarre, so painful, so humiliating . . . yet so joyous."

—*Ken Green*

"Golf is just the comedy side of what's going
on in life. But, hey, this world is great.
You can make fun of anything, from the
tensest moments to the not so tense.
Golf is a pressure game where funny
and crazy things happen."

_Billy Andrade

◆

"Golf is like real estate, where there's a
single key word: location, location, location.
In golf it's putting, putting, putting."

_David Ogrin

"Golf—the second best pastime
that any sinner on this earth can have."

—Sportswriter R. H. Lyttleton

◆

"Golf is a game where guts, stick-to-itiveness
and blind devotion will always net you
absolutely nothing but an ulcer."

—Tommy Bolt

◆

"They say that life is a lot like golf—
don't believe them. Golf is a lot
more complicated."

—Gardner Dickinson

"Golf is the worst drug in the world.
You just keep coming back for
more embarrassment."

—Former NFL great Deacon Jones

◆

"Golf is like any other sports competition.
There is not a whole lot of point to it
unless someone suffers."

—Golf writer Kevin Wohl

◆

"Golf is 90 percent inspiration
and 10 percent perspiration."

—Johnny Miller

"Golf is a lot like sex. Even when you cheat you still have to get it up and in. And that gets tougher and tougher to do every year."

_Billy Orville

◆

"Golf is played by 20 million mature American men whose wives think they are out there having fun."

_Columnist Jim Bishop

The Pros

"Walter Hagen had a sterling contempt for second place. He believed that the public only remembered a winner, that a man might as well be tenth as second when the shooting was over."

—Golf writer Herbert Warren Wind

"I see no reason why a golf course cannot be played in 18 birdies. Just because no one has ever done that doesn't mean it can't be done."

—Ben Hogan

"If golfers can run around and crow
when they make a birdie, I think it would be
just as proper to lie down on the green
and cry when you make a bogey."

–J. C. Snead

◆

"How long does John Daly drive a golf ball?
When I was a kid, I didn't go that far
on vacation."

–Chi Chi Rodriguez

"TV wants a couple of marquee names in the final, but that may not happen. Upsets happen in the NCAA tournament and in tennis all the time. They can happen in match-play golf, too."

—Shigeki Maruyama, on his emergence on the PGA Tour

◆

"I'll never forget that day. What I can't remember is how I did it!"

—Jose Maria Olazabal, nine years after scoring a course-record 61 at the formidable Firestone Country Club in Akron, Ohio

"He never brought his golf home. At dinner he'd ask us how we did at school. We'd pick up a newspaper and see that he'd won something."

Janice Salvi, daughter of Francis Ouimet, winner of the 1913 U.S. Open

◆

"When Jack Nicklaus plays well, he wins. When he plays badly, he finishes second. When he plays terribly, he finishes third."

Johnny Miller

"He basically felt like he had killed my dog
or something."

_Fred Couples, recounting a talk with Ben Crenshaw, the
Ryder Cup captain who left him off the 1999 squad

◆

"He's a genius, but it's definitely a flawed genius.
You know that quote about how God doesn't
give you everything? With Monty, it's the
inability to control himself at given moments."

_Swing coach Denis Pugh, on moody Scotsman
Colin Montgomerie

"Every once in a while, you see Tiger Woods
and David Duval playing the way they've played
and you think it's easy to win.
It's just not that easy."

_Paul Azinger

◆

"You kind of play up to your competition.
You're playing with the best players in the world,
and your concentration and your focus
goes to the next level."

_1997 U.S. Amateur Champion Matt Kuchar,
on finishing 21st against pros at the 1998 Masters
and 14th at the 1998 U.S. Open

"The reality of life as a pro golfer is that the difference between a good day and a bad day is just a spin of the ball."

—LPGA player Kathryn Marshall

◆

"I asked Mark on the first tee what I needed to shoot to make the team and he said '45.'"

—European Tour player Russell Claydon, after chatting with European Ryder Cup captain Mark James before the 1999 BMW International

"Tiger is the dragon out here.
Somebody had to slay him."

*—Jeff Maggert, after squeaking by Woods to win the 1999
Andersen Consulting Match Play Championship*

◆

"Who's caught up with Tiger?
Who is this person? I haven't met him yet.
All it looks like to me is Tiger is catching up
with God."

—Paul Goydos, on Tiger Woods

"It was a contest to see who could play the ugliest today, and I won . . . the contest, not the match."

_Stewart Cink, after blowing a lead

MOST WRETCHED GOLFER

"It's always hard to sleep when you got a big early lead. You just lie there and smile at the ceiling all night."

Dave Stockton

◆

"Ben Hogan would rather have a coral snake rolling inside his shirt than hit a hook."

Claude Harmon

◆

"Somebody asked me once, 'Who's better? Jack Nicklaus or Ben Hogan?' Well, my answer was, 'I saw Nicklaus watch Hogan practice. But I never saw Hogan watch Nicklaus.'"

Tommy Bolt

"Michael Jordan strikes me as one of the greatest athletes who ever lived, but Sam Snead still goes down as the greatest. He's performed in his teens, his twenties, his thirties, his forties, his fifties, his sixties, and at seventy he finished second."

—Gary Player

◆

"When you step on the first tee it doesn't matter what you look like. Being pretty, ugly, or semi-ugly has no effect on the golf ball. It doesn't hurt your five-iron if you're pretty."

—Laura Baugh, on being complimented for her good looks

"You can flop it up there and look like a hero, but it is all luck."

_Tiger Woods, on the art of the chip shot

◆

"I have been fined many times on the European Tour. They are trying to become rich because of me."

_Often-fined Sergio Garcia

◆

"Nicklaus is definitely God 1, Watson is God 2, Palmer is God 3, Ballesteros is God 4. I got so close to Jack, I almost got religious."

_A caddie at the 1984 British Open

"Gray-blue, they had a piercing quality. They were the eyes of a circling bird of prey: fearless, fierce, the pupil no more than a dot in their imperious center. They were not the eyes of a loser."

—*Sportswriter Jim Murray, on the eyes of Ben Hogan*

◆

"People are great, and I try to acknowledge them as much as I can. They're the ones who make things happen so we can do what we do for a living. Without their support, we're just playing in front of trees and squirrels."

—*Fuzzy Zoeller*

"That didn't really happen. It was a mirage. It was weird, like the whole thing wasn't happening."

_Johnny Miller, after winning the 1994 AT&T Pebble Beach National Pro-Am

◆

"The only thing that can stop him is an injury or a bad marriage."

_Writer Dan Jenkins, on Tiger Woods

◆

"He's playing a game I'm not familiar with. Of course, I'm playing a game I'm not familiar with."

_Jack Nicklaus, on playing partner Tiger Woods in 2000

"I don't know if he has to talk about me
in his press conferences, but I definitely have
to talk about him."

_Karrie Webb, on being compared constantly to Tiger Woods

◆

"It wouldn't make a bloody bit of difference.
I would just get bored."

_Laura Davies, on whether more practice would help her
against rival Karrie Webb

◆

"Where's Tonya Harding when you need her?"

_Scott Hoch, after getting walloped by David Duval

"I didn't want to be the bad guy. I wasn't trying to end the streak per se. I was just trying to win the golf tournament."

_Phil Mickelson, after beating Tiger Woods at the 2000 Buick Invitational

◆

"There are five top superstars in golf, 20 great stars, and 30 good ones. The rest should go and get jobs."

_International Management Group CEO Mark McCormick

"Golf fairways should be made more narrow.
Then everyone would have to play from
the rough, not just me."

—Seve Ballesteros

◆

"What makes a great captain? Twelve great
players. My job is to get them matched up
and motivate them so they make me look good.
If they play good, we all look great.
If they don't, I look dumb."

*—Curtis Strange, after being elected
U.S. Ryder Cup captain in 1999*

"If you like root canals and hemorrhoids,
you'd love it there."

—Nick Price, describing the Ryder Cup experience

◆

"I'll have to go shopping. I don't think
I have any more clean shirts."

*—Mark McCumber, after making his first
PGA Tour cut in two years at the 1999 Honda Classic*

◆

"If it was good enough for Hogan,
it's good enough for me."

*—Steve Elkington, on why he hadn't switched
from metal to alternate spikes*

"On paper, they should be caddying for us.
But that isn't what this is about.
It's about bringing your game to the event . . .
and they bring it."

_1999 U.S. Ryder Cup member Payne Stewart,
sizing up the European squad

◆

"I'm a big believer in fate . . . I have a good
feeling about this."

_U.S. Ryder Cup captain Ben Crenshaw, the night before
his struggling squad overcame a record-setting four-point
deficit to beat the Europeans in 1999

"Our guys went halfway around the world to Australia to play against a bunch of guys from Orlando."

_Lanny Wadkins, on the 1998 President's Cup that pitted top American players against Australia's best . . . many of whom had homes in Florida

◆

"You've got a fairly good idea as to what the questions are going to be. But how to record the best answer is another matter."

_Nick Faldo, comparing the U.S. Open to an exam

"The change was really kind of nice
because the most embarrassing thing
was when one of those Generation Xers
would come up and ask who Dinah Shore was."

—*Dottie Pepper, on the renaming of the Nabisco Dinah
Shore to the Nabisco Championship*

◆

"There's no reason to compare apples to oranges.
But this is one hell of an orange."

—*Justin Leonard, when asked to compare the
British Open and the Players Championship*

"I've got a lot to think about—
and all weekend to think about it."

_David Duval, after missing his first cut in two years

◆

"The fact that I didn't win an eighth
Order of Merit was probably what saved
my marriage."

_Colin Montgomerie, blaming pressure of his golf career
with nearly wrecking his family life

"I was the world's worst salesman."

_Joe Durant, on why he gave pro golf another chance

◆

"Golf is a game of days, and I can
beat anyone on my day."

_Fuzzy Zoeller

◆

"Today was almost better than sex . . . almost."

_Per-Ulrik Johansson, after shooting a 64

"I don't know . . . I never played there."

—Sandy Lyle, when asked what he thought of Tiger Woods

◆

"There is no love lost in match play."

—Craig Stadler, after a 1999 match in which he refused to concede putts of 18 inches and three feet to Colin Montgomerie

Declarations,
Proclamations,
and Observations

"Any person who shall wear to a golfing event any device or thing attached to his or her head, hair, headgear, or hat, which device or thing is capable of lacerating the flesh of anyone with whom it may come in contact and which is not sufficiently guarded against the possibility of doing so, shall be adjudged a disorderly person."

—Wilmington, North Carolina, city ordinance

◆

"I don't view golf as a substitute for formal worship, but I do believe God is present and can be experienced on the golf course."

—Clergyman Paul Reitman, who taught a four-week college course entitled "The Spirituality of Golf"

"No male golfer shall make remarks to or concerning, or cough or whistle at, or do any other act to attract the attention of any woman golfer."

—Local ordinance in Tucson, Arizona

"Lord, God of all creation, we bless You for Your grass and trees, and sand and water, but mostly for Your golf courses. We praise You for the birdies You have made to fly, and beg of You more birdies that are made to drop. If this request o'ersteps the bounds to 'ask and you will receive,' we shall be grateful still for plentiful pars. Deliver us from all bogeys, double or simply single. Amen."

—FROM TEE TO GREEN, *a golfer's prayer book composed by the Reverend Michael Lawler*

"Constitutionally and physically women are unfitted for golf. The first women's championship will be the last . . . They are bound to fall out and quarrel on the slightest, or no, provocation."

—Nineteenth-century golf writer Horace Hutchinson, upon hearing the Ladies Golf Union of England was trying to organize a major tournament in 1893

◆

"If you ask me, I don't think anything should be illegal . . . golf equipment, that is."

—John Daly

"Give me a man with big hands,
big feet, and no brains,
and I will make a golfer out of him."

—Walter Hagen

◆

"Strictly speaking, there is nothing to stop a
player from carrying a ladder around with him—
although that might not be the image the
Tour wants to project."

*—European Tour official John Paramor, after a player
borrowed a ladder from a TV crew to scale a palm tree and
identify his ball during the 1998 Spanish Open*

"Stroke play is my second favorite form of golf, and by quite a long way. It is not the play itself that puts me off, it is the task of marking a card."

_Writer Peter Dobereiner

◆

"The hardest part was getting in and out of the car and buckling and unbuckling the seatbelt 90 times."

_Don "Snowshoe" Thompson, after hitting a ball at 44 courses in one 12-hour stretch

"We'll wed at the blues, tee off at the reds, and honeymoon in Carmel Valley, golfing all the way."

—Sportswriter Susan Fornoff, before her wedding at the seventh tee at San Francisco's Bodega Harbour Golf Links

◆

"If that guy ever wins a tournament, it will set golf back 100 years."

—PGA champ Chick Harbert, watching newcomer Arnold Palmer at the 1954 U.S. Amateur

"Gary, lad, what you want to do is go home to Johannesburg, forget about golf, and get yourself an honest job."

Advice given to Gary Player, after the future Hall of Famer missed the cut at a 1955 tournament

◆

"I got the last laugh on him."

Nick Faldo, recalling the youth employment officer who ridiculed him as a teen for wanting to become a pro golfer

"Daddy, am I ready to beat the ladies?"

—*Nancy Lopez, at age 11, just before winning three consecutive New Mexico Women's Amateur titles*

◆

"Latest to join the professional ranks is
Arnold Palmer, national amateur champion.
Not the least interesting piece of personal data
to young ladies is that he is a bachelor."

—*Glib welcome* GOLF WORLD *gave the future legend in 1954*

"He's hit it fat . . . It will probably be short . . .
It just hit the front edge of the green . . . It's got
no chance . . . It's rolling, but it will stop . . .
It's rolling toward the cup . . . Well, I'll be
goddamned, he sank it!"

_TV announcer Jimmy Demaret, calling a
104-yard eagle shot

◆

"You'll never get anywhere fooling around
those golf courses."

_Clara Hogan's advice to son Ben

"He hit a flaming whoopsie into the coconuts."

_Golf analyst David Feherty, describing an errant tee shot

◆

"Work puts a negative connotation
on practicing."

_Tom Kite

◆

"Someone who turns up at the first tee
on time and sober."

_Ernie Els, on what makes a good caddie

Bad Lies

"There are certain things you don't believe in. The Easter Bunny. Campaign promises. The Abominable Snowman. A husband with lipstick on his collar. And a guy who tells you he shot a 59 on his own ball. Out of town, of course."

—Columnist Jim Murray

◆

"I think after four hours you should pick your ball up and walk in, and if you haven't finished, that's tough."

—Colin Montgomerie

"Golf is the hardest game in the world to play
and the easiest to cheat at."

_Dave Hill

◆

"If there is any larceny in a man,
golf will bring it out."

_Writer Paul Gallico

◆

"Golf is a game where the ball always
lies poorly and the player well."

_Anonymous

"The biggest liar in the world is the golfer
who claims that he plays the game merely
for exercise."

—Tommy Bolt

◆

"Golf does strange things to other people too.
It makes liars out of honest men,
cheats out of altruists, cowards out of brave men,
and fools out of everybody."

—Sportswriter Milton Gross

◆

"Golf is like solitaire. When you cheat,
you cheat only yourself."

—Tony Lema

"The difference between golf and the government is that in golf you can't improve your lie."

_Former California Governor George Deukmejian

◆

"You know the old rule: He who have fastest cart never have to play bad lie."

_Baseball Hall of Famer Mickey Mantle

◆

"Golf is a game in which you yell fore, shoot six, and write down five."

_Radio personality Paul Harvey

"Golf is based on honesty. Where else would you admit to a seven on a par three?"

—Jimmy Demaret

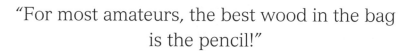

"For most amateurs, the best wood in the bag is the pencil!"

—Chi Chi Rodriguez

"The devil invented golf, so the least we can do
is return the favor and cheat like hell
when we play."

—THE GOLFER'S HOME COMPANION

◆

"Golf could be our national sport
before very long."

*—Denis Hzerebko, president of the
Federation of Professional Golfers in Russia—
a country with one golf course in the year 2000*

Politics of Golf

"If I had my way, any man guilty of golf would be ineligible for any office of trust in the United States."

_Humorist H. L. Mencken

◆

"If everybody in Washington in government service who belongs or has belonged to a restricted golf club was to leave government service, this city would have the highest rate of unemployment of any city in the country."

_President Richard Nixon

"I know I'm getting better at golf because I'm hitting fewer spectators. Either that, or fewer people are watching me play."

_President Gerald Ford

"At least he can't cheat on his score
because all you have to do is look back
down the fairway and count the wounded."

—Comedian Bob Hope, about wild-swinging Gerald Ford

◆

"It's amazing how many people beat you at golf
now that you're no longer president."

—President George Bush

◆

"President [George] Bush does not take
mulligans. That family plays by the rules."

—Ben Crenshaw

"By the time you get dressed, drive out there, play 18 holes, and come home, you've blown seven hours. There are better things you can do with your time."

—President Richard Nixon

"I deny allegations by Bob Hope that during my last game I hit an eagle, a birdie, an elk, and a moose."

—President Gerald Ford

"One lesson you better learn if you want
to be in politics is that you never go out
and beat the president."

—President Lyndon Johnson

◆

"Either he is an unbelievable athlete
or I have a career as a golf instructor."

*—President Bill Clinton, after guiding British Prime Minister
Tony Blair through his first-ever round of golf*

"Rail-splitting produced an immortal president in Abraham Lincoln; but golf, with 29,000 courses, hasn't produced even a good A-Number-1 congressman."

_Humorist Will Rogers

"If I swung the gavel the way I swung that golf club, the nation would be in a helluva mess."

_Former Speaker of the U.S. House of Representatives Tip O'Neill

◆

"I would have been worried if they played well. It would have meant they were spending too much time playing golf and not enough time running the country."

_Seve Ballesteros, after teaming with Portugal's president and minister of justice to finish last at a pro-am event

"I don't have any handicap. I am all handicap."

_President Lyndon Johnson

◆

"Mr. Agnew, I believe you have a
slight swing in your flaw."

_Jimmy Demaret, to playing partner
Vice President Spiro Agnew

◆

"Golf is a fine relief from the tensions of office,
but we are a little tired of holding the bag."

_Presidential contender Adlai Stevenson

Money Talks

"If I'm going to play golf, I might as well play for the money."

—*Arnold Palmer, upon turning pro in 1954*

"Never bet with anyone you meet on the first tee who has a deep sunburn, a one-iron in his bag, and squinty eyes."

—*Dave Marr*

"Guarantee me three million dollars a year and you can scream, yell, or spit on my ball when I'm putting. Because even if I miss, I get paid."

—*Lee Trevino*

"It's nice to have the opportunity to play for so much money, but it's nicer to win it."

_Patty Sheehan, on the increasing purses in the LPGA

◆

"The players themselves can be classified into two groups—the attractions and the entry fees."

_Jimmy Demaret

◆

"Let's see, I think right now I'm third in money-winning and first in money-spending."

_Tony Lema

"Give me a millionaire with a bad backswing and I can have a very pleasant afternoon."

—Legendary hustler George Low Jr.

◆

"If I could change one thing about the Tour it would be the size of the purses. It's hard to support a family playing full time."

—Dick Mast, at the 1990 Ben Hogan New Haven Open

◆

"I never wanted to be a millionaire. I just wanted to live like one."

—Walter Hagen

"When you play the game for fun, it's fun. When you play it for a living, it's a game of sorrows."

—Gary Player

◆

"The dollars aren't so important . . . once you have them."

—Johnny Miller

◆

"We're going to have a lot more gray hair, but the thing that isn't going to change is that the same good players are going to make all the money."

—Dana Quigley, on the tough conditions of a 2001 Senior PGA Tour tourney

No Putts About It

"You get no points for style when it comes to putting. It's getting the ball to drop into the cup that counts."

—Scottish golfer Laurie Auchterlonie

◆

"You drive for show and putt for dough."

—Al Balding

◆

"I have three-putted in 40 countries."

—Fred Corcoran

◆

"If you're going to miss 'em, miss 'em quick."

—George Duncan, on his quick style of putting

"Selecting a putter is like selecting a wife:
To each his own."

—Ben Hogan

◆

"You have to put your putter out to pasture
every so often, let it eat and get fat
so it can get more birdies."

—Greg Norman

◆

"Putting is my weak spot and always
leaves me ripping. My other two weaknesses
are the driving and the chipping."

—Humorist Arnold Zarett

"Around the clubhouse they'll tell you
even God has to practice his putting.
In fact, even Nicklaus does."

—Sportswriter Jim Murray

◆

"Putting is like wisdom—partly a natural gift
and partly the accumulation of experience."

—Arnold Palmer

◆

"Putts get real difficult
the day they hand out the money."

—Lee Trevino

"I never really dreamed of making many putts. Maybe that's why I haven't made many."

_Calvin Peete

◆

"In golf, driving is a game of free-swinging muscle control, while putting is something like performing eye surgery and using a bread knife for a scalpel."

_Tommy Bolt

◆

"Prayer never seems to work for me on the golf course. I think this has something to do with my being a terrible putter."

_The Reverend Billy Graham

"Ninety percent of putts that are short
don't go in."

_Baseball great Yogi Berra

◆

"I'm putting so badly, I could putt it off a tabletop
and leave it short halfway down a leg."

_J. C. Snead

◆

"What greater calamity can befall a golfer than
a short putt missed? What greater averter of
calamity could there be than a long putt holed?"

_BROWNING'S HISTORY OF GOLF

"The way I putted, I must have been reading the greens in Spanish and putting them in English."

—Mexican-born Senior Tour pro Homero Blancas

"The ball's got to stop somewhere. It might as well be in the bottom of the hole."

—Lee Trevino, on his aggressive putting stroke

◆

"It's a marriage. If I had to choose between my wife and my putter, well, I'd miss her."

—Gary Player

◆

"I curse the day the head of my putter fell off. It's kind of like losing one of your best friends."

—Nick Price

"That putt was so good
I could hear the baby applaud."

_Donna Horton White, after holing a 25-foot putt
while seven months pregnant

"Putting is a game unto itself. If I could putt,
I could win."

_Tom Watson

Golf Truisms

"The more you play golf,
the less you know about it."

LPGA Hall of Famer Patty Berg

◆

"When you fall in love with golf, you seldom
fall easy. It's obsession at first sight."

Sportswriter Thomas Boswell

◆

"Murphy's first law of golf:
You can't lose an old ball!"

Columnist John Willis

"Your best shots in golf are your
practice swing and the conceded putt.
You'll never master the rest!"

—NATO Secretary General Lord Robertson

◆

"Playing golf is like raising children:
You keep thinking you'll do better next time."

—Author E. C. McKenzie

◆

"Golf practice—something you do to convert
a nasty hook into a wicked slice."

—Humorist Henry Beard

"The only shots you can be dead sure of
are those you've already taken."

_Byron Nelson

◆

"It is nothing new or original to say that
golf is played one stroke at a time.
But it took me many years to realize it."

_Bobby Jones

◆

"The uglier a man's legs are, the better
he plays golf. It's almost a law."

_Science fiction writer H. G. Wells

"It has been observed that
absolute idiots play the steadiest golf."

—Nineteenth-century golf writer Sir Walter Simpson

"Learning to play golf is like learning to play
the violin. It's not only difficult to do,
it's very painful to everyone around you."

—Actor Hal Linden

"The only thing a golfer needs is more daylight."

—Ben Hogan, on cutting-edge equipment

"You can be the greatest iron player in the world or the greatest putter, but if you can't get the ball in position to use your greatness, you can't win."

—Ben Hogan

◆

"Local rules in golf—a set of regulations that are ignored by players on a specific course rather than by golfers as a whole."

—Humorist Roy McKie

◆

"You can talk to a fade, but a hook won't listen."

—Lee Trevino

"Talking to a golf ball won't do you any good.
Unless you do it while your opponent is
teeing off."

—Author Bruce Lansky

◆

"The harder you work, the luckier you get."

—Gary Player

◆

"Always throw your clubs ahead of you.
That way you don't have to waste energy
going back to pick them up."

—Tommy Bolt

"Thinking instead of acting is the
number-one golf disease."

_Sam Snead

"The fun you get from golf is in direct ratio
to the effort you don't put into it."

_Comedian Bob Allen

"If you want to beat someone out on the
golf course, just get him mad."

_Collegiate golf coach Dave Williams

"The number-one thing about trouble is . . .
don't get into more."

Dave Stockton

◆

"Nothing goes down slower than a
golf handicap."

Bobby Nichols

◆

"The world's number-one tennis player spends
90 percent of his time winning, while the world's
number-one golfer spends 90 percent of his
time losing. Golfers are great losers."

David Feherty

"A driving range is the place where golfers
go to get all the good shots out of their system."

_Humorist Henry Beard

"Golfers find it a very trying matter
to turn at the waist, more particularly
if they have a lot of waist to turn."

_Harry Vardon

"Great southpaw golfers are more scarce
than a clean day in Los Angeles."

_Golf writer Joe Schwendeman

"The most exquisitely satisfying act in the world of golf is that of throwing a club. The full backswing, the delayed wrist action, the flowing follow-through, followed by that unique whirring sound, reminiscent only of a passing flock of starlings, are without parallel in sport."

—Golf writer Henry Longhurst

"Do not be tempted to invest in a sample of each golfing invention as soon as it makes its appearance. If you do, you will only complicate and spoil your game—and encumber your locker with useless rubbish."

—Harry Vardon

◆

"A perfect spectator must have the eye of an eagle, the neck of a giraffe, the skin of an alligator, and the bladder of an elephant."

—Winning entry for newspaper contest of "a perfect spectator"

"Two things that ain't long for this world—dogs that chase cars and professional golfers who chip for pars."

—Lee Trevino

◆

"The toughest thing I've ever had to do in golf is hit the ball off that first tee with thousands of people watching and having no idea where the ball was going."

—Byron Nelson

◆

"Nothing dissects a man in public quite like golf."

—Sportscaster Brent Musberger

"A perfectly straight shot with a big club
is a fluke!"

—Jack Nicklaus

◆

"Practice puts brains in your muscles."

—Sam Snead

◆

"Show me someone who gets angry once in a
while, and I'll show you a guy with a killer
instinct. Show me a guy walking down the
fairway smiling, and I'll show you a loser."

—Lee Trevino

"If you travel first class, you think first class and you are more likely to play first class."

_Ray Floyd

◆

"All good players have good hands. And I'm afraid you have to be born with them."

_Dave Stockton

◆

"You're a good loser if you can grip the winner's hand without wishing it was his throat."

_Sportswriter Hal Chadwick

"Victory is everything. You can spend the money, but you can never spend the memories."

—Ken Venturi

◆

"Golf and sex are about the only things you can enjoy without being good at it."

—Jimmy Demaret

◆

"It's funny . . . you need a fantastic memory in this game to remember the great shots and a very short memory to forget the bad ones."

—Gary McCord

"The player may experiment about his swing, his grip, his stance. It is only when he begins asking his caddie's advice that he is getting on dangerous ground."

_Nineteenth-century golf writer Sir Walter Simpson

◆

"If you're stupid enough to whiff, you should be smart enough to forget it."

_Arnold Palmer

◆

"We tell our stories of hard-luck shots, of each shot straight and true. But when we are through, remember, old boy, nobody cares but you."

_Walter Hagen

"Many shots are spoiled at the last instant by efforts to add a few more yards."

_Bobby Jones

◆

"There is no such thing as a natural touch. Touch is something you create by hitting millions of golf balls."

_Lee Trevino

◆

"The difference between getting in a sand trap and getting in water is like the difference between an auto wreck and an airplane wreck. You can recover from one of them."

_Bobby Jones

"Having a great golf swing helps under pressure, but golf is a game about scoring. It's like an artist who can get a two-inch brush at Wal-Mart for 20 cents or a fine camel-hair brush from an art store for 20 dollars. The brush doesn't matter—how the finished painting looks is what matters."

—Jerry Pate

◆

"If you're playing well, they could probably put the pin on the cart path and you'd get it close."

—Mike Sullivan

"The good chip allows you to whistle while you walk in the dark alleys of golf."

—Tommy Bolt

◆

"When the ducks are walking, you know it is too windy to be playing golf."

—Dave Stockton

◆

"Serenity is knowing that your worst shot is still gonna be pretty good."

—Johnny Miller

"The real success in golf lies in turning three shots into two."

—Bobby Locke

"Man blames fate for other accidents but feels personally responsible for a hole in one."

—Writer Martha Beckman

The Senior Circuit

"When you get this old, you wake up with a different pain each day. Besides, it's a grind trying to beat 60-year-old kids out there."

_Sam Snead, 80, on his decision to skip the Senior Tour

◆

"Having sucked the orange dry, I see no reason to eat the peel."

_Peter Alliss, on why he nixed playing on the Senior Tour

◆

"Like a lot of fellows on the Senior Tour, I have a furniture problem: My chest has fallen into my drawers."

_Billy Casper

"Old golfers never die. They just putter away."

—Anonymous

◆

"What's so nice about our tours is that you can't remember your bad shots."

—Bobby Brue

◆

"I went to bed on September 4, 1992, and I was old and washed up. I woke up a rookie. What could be better?"

—Raymond Floyd, on turning 50 and becoming eligible for the Senior Tour

"One of the nice things about the Senior Tour is that we can take a cart and cooler. If your game is not going well, you can always have a picnic."

_Lee Trevino

◆

"The way I played last week, the LPGA would have whipped my butt."

_Tom Watson, after finishing tied for 22nd in his 1999 Senior Tour debut

"My game is so bad I've got to hire three caddies—one to walk the left rough, one for the right rough, and one down the middle. And the one in the middle doesn't have much to do."

—Dave Hill

"Once, 70 used to be his score. On a bad day. Now it's his age. But as long as he's out there ready to make a charge, he'll never grow old."

—Columnist Art Spander on Arnold Palmer, who turned 70 in 1999

"I think I just got better with age.
Maybe I wasn't ready to handle it before.
The other tour is work. This is more fun."

_Bruce Fleisher, after winning the Transamerica Seniors event
in 1999, the sixth win of his rookie season compared to just
one title in 408 starts on the PGA Tour

◆

"Maybe somebody channeled my body.
Maybe Tiger was channeled in. I'll blame it
on something . . . something extraterrestrial."

_Gary McCord, after winning his first
Senior Tour title in 1999

"It's one thing to meet the devil.
It's another thing to see him coming."

_Chi Chi Rodriguez, on Tom Watson's
senior circuit debut in 1999

◆

"Somebody is going to wake up one
morning and realize the Senior Tour is not
a bunch of over-the-hill guys."

_Hale Irwin

◆

"Billy Casper has won titles at more
weight levels than Sugar Ray Leonard."

_John Brodie, on the yo-yoing weight of
his fellow senior golfer

"My game is not for display right now. I do, however, get great pleasure from playing and replaying holes in my mind."

—Ben Hogan, on retirement

◆

"I won't say my golf is bad, but if I started growing tomatoes, they'd come up sliced!"

—Miller Barber

◆

"I'm hitting the woods just great, but I'm having a helluva time gettin' out of them."

—Club pro Henry Toscano

"Somebody give me a banana. I'm playing like a monkey, so I might as well eat like one."

_Chi Chi Rodriguez, during a bad Senior Tour round

"Old-time golfers insist that there is nothing more satisfying in the game of golf than the crisp snap of a hickory-shafted club breaking sharply across the player's knee."

—Humorist Henry Beard

◆

"Some of these Legends of Golf have been around golf for a long time. When they talk about having a good grip, they're talking about their dentures."

—Comedian Bob Hope

"He wasn't a great ballplayer, but he always tried very hard. I would run around saying I am Chi Chi Flores, and pretty soon people started calling me Chi Chi."

—Chi Chi Rodriguez, on getting his famous nickname

◆

"Never have I done anything this idiotic in my career . . . if there's one thing that could drive me back to drink, this is it."

—British golfer Brian Barnes, after his ball-marking blunder cost him the 1998 U.S. Senior Open

"I can't believe I missed a good
stock car race for this."

—*Larry Ziegler, after watching Hale Irwin win the 1998*
U.S. Senior Open with a one-over-par 285

◆

"If this tour is a blood bank, he's going to be a
Count Dracula having a gory feast."

—*TV announcer Gary McCord, on Tom Watson's*
Senior Tour debut

◆

"Being a left-hander is a big advantage.
No one knows enough about your game
to mess you up with advice."

—*Southpaw senior golfer Bob Charles*

"I sure was glad I ran out of holes. I looked down at my hands and arms to see if it was me when I finished with the score."

—Don January, after a poor Senior Tour round

◆

"After caddying for Jack, I thought I would never meet anyone who is more intense, but now I have. I'm not calling Hale a better player than Jack, but he is definitely more of a competitor. He absolutely cannot stand to hit a bad shot, even in a pro-am."

—Former Jack Nicklaus caddie John Sullivan, on Hale Irwin

"I've been doing the sword dance for pars because I don't make enough birdies. That's when I know my game has gone bad."

_Chi Chi Rodriquez, during a Senior Tour slump in 1996

◆

"Man, this is one of them airport drivers. That's right. You hit this thing for two days, miss the cut, and go to the airport."

_Lee Trevino, wielding a fellow senior's old club

"The people were just great. They put up with my horrendous golf."

_Arnold Palmer, after finishing 74th at the 1999 BankBoston Classic

◆

"Now I can see I can't make anything."

_Jack Nicklaus, on his new contact lenses

Grand Slams
of Golf

"They call it golf because all of the other four-letter words were taken."

—Raymond Floyd

◆

"Can you name me one single case where devotion to this pestilential pastime has done a man any practical good?"

—Humorist P. G. Wodehouse

◆

"Golf is an open exhibition of overweening ambition, courage deflated by stupidity, and skill soured by a whiff of arrogance."

—Journalist Alistair Cooke

"If you want to take long walks, take long walks. If you want to hit things with a stick, hit things with a stick. But there's no excuse for combining the two and putting the results on TV. Golf is not so much a sport as an insult to lawns."

—NATIONAL LAMPOON

◆

"Playing golf is like chasing a quinine pill around a cow pasture."

—British Prime Minister Winston Churchill

◆

"I don't care to join any club that's prepared to have me as a member."

—Comedian Groucho Marx

"I do not remember any golfer who did not consider himself, on the whole, a remarkably unlucky one."

—Nineteenth-century golf writer Sir Walter Simpson

◆

"If profanity had any influence on the flight of the ball, the game would be played far better than it is."

—Nineteenth-century golf writer Horace G. Hutchinson

◆

"Golf had humbled, humiliated, and just about licked all the great athletes I ever knew that tried it."

—Football coach Earl "Red" Blaik

"The most advanced medical brains
in the universe have yet to discover a way
for a man to relax himself, and looking at
a golf ball is not the cure."

_Author Milton Gross

◆

"I guess there is nothing that will get your mind
off everything like golf will. I have never been
depressed enough to take up the game, but they
say you can get so sore at yourself that you
forget to hate your enemies."

_Humorist Will Rogers

"There are now more golf clubs in the world than Gideon Bibles, more golf balls than missionaries, and, if every golfer in the world, male and female, were laid end to end, I, for one, would leave them there."

—Michael Parkinson, president of the Anti-Golf Society

◆

"Excessive golfing dwarfs the intellect. And this is to be wondered at, when we consider that the more fatuously vacant the mind is, the better for play."

—Nineteenth-century golf writer Sir Walter Simpson

"A hundred years of experience has demonstrated that the game is temporary insanity practiced in a pasture."

Columnist Dave Kindred

"These young fellows are so completely wrapped up in getting a little golf ball into a little hole in less strokes than anyone else that their attitude and sense of intelligent balance to the more important things in life have not only been distorted, but are practically nonexistent. The young man careerists are not the only offenders; the young lady careerists are just as bad."

_Course designer Donald Ross, in 1914

◆

"I played nine holes with the new short-distance ball. Playing a match with it is like two boxers fighting with pillows."

_Sam Snead

"There is not the slightest doubt in my mind that golf—as played in the United States— is the slowest in the world."

_Sportswriter Henry Longhurst

◆

"When I come back in the next life, I want to come back as a golf pro's wife. She wakes up every morning at the crack of 10 and is faced with her first major decision of the day: whether to have breakfast in bed or in the hotel coffee shop."

_Dan Sikes

"It wasn't dangerous enough. I'd rather be in the gallery and get hit by a ball."

—Comedian Jerry Seinfeld, on his one and only round of golf

◆

"The clubs were not the problem. My brain was."

—Payne Stewart, on his poor 1994 season

◆

"I'm fired? I didn't even know I was working for her."

—Golf instructor Butch Harmon, after being informed he'd been fired by Se Ri Pak

"I don't want to say Colin Montgomerie and Darren Clarke are big, but if you took a picture of them together from behind, it would look like one of these double greens."

—*Steve Elkington*

◆

"If you had a bunch of caddies and pros and after three holes they went around the corner and switched clothes, you couldn't tell who was who."

—*Doug Sanders, lamenting the conservative attire of today's players*

"If the U.S. Ryder Cup team got washed up on a desert island, they would build 12 separate huts and go off and grill their own swordfish."

Columnist Martin Johnson, criticizing the "one-for-one" attitude of American pros

◆

"Looks like Generation X is turning into Generation Selfish."

Lanny Wadkins, on the 1999 Ryder Cup controversy over player compensation

◆

"Out here, guys bitch about everything. They even bitch about the ice cream."

Ed Dougherty, on the PGA Tour

"The kids on the Tour today are too good at losing. Show me a 'good loser' and I'll show you a 'seldom winner.'"

—Sam Snead

◆

"You've let your family down, you've let your town down . . . in fact, you've let your country down."

—James Montgomerie, to his son Colin after the latter fired a 76 at the 1997 British Open

◆

"I looked up the word *patience* in an Irish dictionary . . . and it wasn't there."

—Bob Murphy

"Sportswriters—professionals with no known minimum standard—are paid to stand in judgment over a professional golfer, making fun of his mistakes and impugning his character, just before they go out on Monday and play the same course in 112 blows. For free."

‑THE GOLFER'S HOME COMPANION

"I think most of the rules of golf stink. They were written by the guys who can't even break a hundred."

‑Chi Chi Rodriguez

"It seems kinda slow. It needs . . .
I don't know . . . it needs defenders or
something."

_NBA guard Jason Williams, on jazzing golf's slow pace

◆

"If you watch a game, it's fun. If you play it, it's
recreation. If you work at it, it's golf."

_Comedian Bob Hope

◆

"Palm Springs is an inland sandbar man has
wrested from the rodents and the Indians to
provide a day camp for overprivileged adults."

_Sportswriter Jim Murray, on the self-proclaimed golf
capital of the world

Self-Exams

"I'm a golfaholic, no question about it. Counseling wouldn't help me. They'd have to put me in prison. And then I'd talk the warden into building a hole or two to teach him how to play."

Lee Trevino

◆

"Every day I try to tell myself that this is going to be fun today. I try to put myself in a great frame of mind before I go out—then I screw it up with the first shot."

Johnny Miller

"Every round I play, I shorten my life
by two years."

_Tommy Nakajima

◆

"I don't like to be honored for anything.
I don't see why anybody makes a big deal out
of a poor little Mexican guy that hits a golf ball
better than most people."

_Lee Trevino

◆

"The game was easy for me as a kid. I had to
play a while to find out how hard it is."

_Raymond Floyd

"I seem to be a target for everything. I must walk around with a dart board on my back."

—Greg Norman, on dodging constant criticism

◆

"I know I can shoot low scores. The challenge is for me to shoot them more often."

—Bruce Lehnard

◆

"I don't consider myself a great black hope. I'm just a golfer who happens to be black and Asian."

—Tiger Woods

"I never played a round when I didn't learn something new about the game."

_Ben Hogan

◆

"I'm not sure that the most talented player I ever saw wasn't myself."

_Johnny Miller

◆

"I don't think television has screwed up my golf. I've pretty much taken care of that on my own."

_Curtis Strange

"There are no guarantees in this game—not to mention this life—and we have only a short time to enjoy it. Even when I'm not playing particularly well, I enjoy what I do."

—Scott Simpson

"I don't resent the media. I get disappointed sometimes. They've got their job to do . . . I've got my job to do. They'll sit back some day in years to come and say, 'Well, geez, I was wrong.' They will. I know they will."

—Greg Norman, on being labeled a professional choker

"I make my living out of golf, but it is still a game to me. When it becomes work and not fun, I'll go into something else."

—Jimmy Demaret

◆

"I may look like a crack dealer, but I'm just trying to be a good parent. If there's a crisis at the day care center while I'm playing, they can reach me."

—Tom Lehman, who wore a pager on his belt during play so he could remain in touch with his toddler son, Thomas

"I play with friends, but we don't play friendly games."

—Ben Hogan

◆

"I probably have forgotten more about golf than I have ever learned."

—Jack Nicklaus

◆

"Overall I hope I can still improve."

—David Duval, after shooting a 59 in the final round to win the 1999 Bob Hope Chrysler Classic

"I never knew what top golf was like until
I turned professional. Then it was too late."

—Steve Melnyk

◆

"They still ask me if I ever think about that putt
I missed to win the 1970 Open at St. Andrews.
I tell them that sometimes it doesn't cross
my mind . . . for a full five minutes."

—Doug Sanders

"I would like to think of myself as an athlete first, but I don't want to do a disservice to the real ones."

David Duval

◆

"I reach over and press down the alarm . . . and I jog to the bathroom."

1999 European Ryder Cup captain Mark James, on his fitness program

"I have a tough time looking at the fans because of the things I've done. I don't look at myself as being good enough to talk to them."

—John Daly, on his career cursed by drinking, gambling, and eating addictions

"I had played poorly for two years and started thinking, 'Gee, maybe I'll do something else.' Then I saw my friends going to work every day and realized that my life wasn't so bad. I've been more patient with my golf since then."

—Steve Pate

"I went from being sick . . . to being thankful for being alive . . . to being happy to be back playing golf . . . to this is no fun being out here and not competing the way I used to."

_Paul Azinger, on seeking the help of a sports psychologist after beating cancer, then suffering sleeplessness, backaches, and headaches in 1999

◆

"I always get a kick out of the guys who say they're getting their game ready to peak at the majors. I'm not that good. Hey, I went into the Masters with low expectations. Look what happened there."

_1998 Masters champ Mark O'Meara

"If I never win a major or never hit another golf ball again, I can look back and say I'm successful. I only need to look at my house to know that. I didn't inherit it . . . I earned it."

_Colin Montgomerie

"I don't do my own golf shirts and I don't do my pants. Pants go to the cleaners, golf shirts to Mom's house. She knows how to do 'em. She knows how to not screw 'em up."

_Justin Leonard, praising mom Nancy's talents

"I don't derive satisfaction from trying to satisfy other people's expectations. I am not out to prove anything to you or to anybody else. I am out to prove it to me."

_World's number two-ranked golfer David Duval, after dropping the 1999 Sprint International to number 72-ranked David Toms

◆

"I'm from the same town as Nancy Lopez and the aliens."

_American Curtis Cup player Jo Jo Robertson, who hails from Roswell, New Mexico, an alleged UFO crash site

"Hopefully my boys will carry on the tradition.
But hopefully not too soon."

_—Scott Spence, who in 1999 began carting his
dead dad's ashes along in his golf bag_

◆

"What I want is to be obscure and happy."

_—British Open champion Ian Baker-Finch,
after retiring in 1998_

◆

"I never hurry, never worry, and always take
time out to smell the flowers along the way."

—Walter Hagen

"No one looks in my bag and says, 'Boy, I like that.' People look in my bag and say, 'Yuck!'"

—Steve Pate, whose clubs included a chromeless, corroded set of irons covered in lead tape

"I can airmail the golf ball a long distance, but sometimes I don't put the right address on it."

—Jim Dent

"I call my sand wedge my 'Half Nelson' because I can always strangle the opposition with it."

—Byron Nelson

"I'm waiting for the day when everything falls into place, when every swing is with confidence, and every shot is exactly what I want. I've been close enough to smell it a couple of times, but I'd like to touch it. Then I think I would be satisfied."

—Tom Watson

◆

"What other people may find in poetry or art museums, I find in the flight of a good drive . . . the white ball sailing up into the blue sky, growing smaller and smaller, then suddenly reaching its apex, curving and falling, finally dropping to the turf to roll some more, just the way I planned it."

—Arnold Palmer

"If it weren't for golf, I'd be waiting on this table instead of sitting at it."

_Judy Rankin, while being honored for her 26 career victories

◆

"I never practice golf.
All it does is louse up my game."

_Orville Moody

◆

"The only reason I played golf was so I could afford to go hunting or fishing."

_Sam Snead

"I've thrown or broken a few clubs in my day. In fact, I guess at one time or another I probably held distance records for every club in the bag."

_Tommy Bolt

◆

"About the only thing left for me is acupuncture—in the brain."

_George Archer

◆

"I tell the lady scorekeepers that if they can hear me cuss, they're standing too close. They've got to realize they're not at a church social."

_Dave Hill

"I don't have any particular hang-ups about superstitions. I did try them all, but they didn't work."

_Kathy Whitworth

"I've joked about how I've survived being struck by lightning. I'm a reject. The Lord didn't want me."

_Lee Trevino

"I've injured both my hands playing golf and they're okay now, but my brain has always been suspect."

_Bob Murphy

"I just love to play golf. I try to play 365 days a year. I don't care if it's January or June. I wanted to play on Christmas Day, but my wife looked at me kind of funny, so I thought I'd better not."

_—Lee Trevino

◆

"I want to win every week. I go to the driving range and bop 'til I drop."

_—Rocky Thompson

◆

"I've had a strange career. I've played every tour around the world—except the ladies' tour."

_—Dick Mast

"I may not be the prettiest girl in the world, but I'd like to see Bo Derek look like a 10 after playing 18 holes of golf in 100-degree weather."

—Jan Stephenson

"I'll sign everything. But please don't shove stuff at me, especially pens. I ruin about 365 shirts a year from pens."

—Arnold Palmer

"I may not swing the prettiest or look the prettiest, and I may do some things kind of funny, but I have a lot of heart."

—Tom Lehman, after winning the 1996 British Open

"My family was so poor they couldn't afford any kids. The lady next door had me."

—Lee Trevino

◆

"I'm fat as it is now. I'd get really fat if I started riding."

—Tim Herron, on having no interest in golf cart accessibility

◆

"My wife doesn't care what I do when I'm away . . . as long as I don't enjoy myself."

—Lee Trevino, on being on the road

"I want my kids to know that they need God in their lives. Sunday is a whole different day when you're on tour. Every Sunday when I get up to play a final round I think, 'Golly, I should be going to church.'"

—*Nancy Lopez, on priorities*

◆

"I played the Tour in 1967 and told jokes and nobody laughed. Then I won the Open the next year, told the same jokes, and everybody laughed like hell."

—*Lee Trevino*

"When I got back from Pebble Beach, people said, 'Good playing, Jack.' When I used to finish sixth in a tournament, people would say, 'Too bad, Jack.' I want to hear that again."

—Jack Nicklaus, after his 1995 sixth-place finish

◆

"You've got to gamble every once in a while in a round of golf. I'm not afraid to screw up."

—Fuzzy Zoeller

◆

"If I had to go play holes or golf courses or golf tournaments that have defeated me in my career, I wouldn't have time for anything else."

—Raymond Floyd

"I don't really do the mowing and gardening.
I leave that to the experts. My part of it is
picking up after the dogs."

_Davis Love III, discussing his role around the house

◆

"Nobody's seen me. I haven't been on television.
I've been going off the 10th tee early in the
morning. I've been playing, literally, in front
of tens and tens of people."

_Tom Kite, on his dismal 1995 season

"With legs as white and bad like mine,
it would be a disastrous thing to see. My wife
hardly lets me wear shorts around the house . . .
It's such an ugly sight."

*—John Paul Cain, on whether players
should wear shorts*

◆

"I have been trying to listen to my heart
more on the golf course when I make decisions
about a shot. However, my heart just isn't
beating loud enough."

—Hale Irwin

"When you talk as fast as I do, you can't choose your words. Whatever flies into my head, I say. Believe me, I've eaten my share of shoes as a result."

—Lee Trevino

◆

"What a shame to waste those great shots on the practice tee. I'd be afraid of finding out what I was doing wrong."

—Walter Hagen, on why he hated to practice

◆

"I'm not going to let the golf interfere with my fishing."

—Tiger Woods

"I'm fat. But other than that,
I'm doing pretty well."

_Steve Pate, offering writers a status report in 2000

◆

"I stayed in shape because I didn't smoke or
drink. I advertised Lucky Strikes, Chesterfields,
and Viceroys, but I never smoked them."

_Sam Snead

◆

"I get all the competition I need in Europe."

_Colin Montgomerie, when asked
why he doesn't play more in America

"I would love to be 16 again. Then again,
I would love to be 58 again."

*—JoAnne Carner, 60, after being asked
about a young opponent*

◆

"I just love American girls. That is a big
attraction for me over here. The girls have
class and are incredibly beautiful. There are
nice girls in Europe, but not too many of them
get to golf events."

—Spanish sensation Sergio Garcia

"One of the ironies of the situation is that I did something wrong, but by taking full responsibilities for my actions, I've gotten a lot of positive feedback. I guess people aren't used to professional athletes owning up to their mistakes."

—Notah Begay III, after being arrested for driving under the influence

◆

"I've lost 2,000 pounds, but I've gained 2,200."

—Billy Casper, on a lifetime battle with his weight

"I'm never satisfied. Trouble is, I want to play like me—and I can't play like me anymore."

—Jack Nicklaus, at the age of 50

◆

"I was a little faster than a snail, but not quite as fast as a turtle."

—Glen Day, describing his pace of play

◆

"The older I get, the better I used to be."

—Lee Trevino

"It could be worse; I could be allergic to beer."

—Greg Norman, on being allergic to grass

◆

"If it weren't for golf,
I'd probably be a caddie today."

—George Archer

Mind Over Matter

"You don't know what pressure is
until you've played for five dollars a hole
with only two in your pocket."

—*Lee Trevino*

◆

"There is nothing—I speak from experience—
in a round of either match or medal competition
that bears down with quite the pressure of
having continually to hole out putts of three
and four feet . . . the kind left by
overly enthusiastic approaches."

—*Bobby Jones*

"My only fear is that I may have to go out and get a real job."

—Fuzzy Zoeller

◆

"The three things I fear the most in golf are lightning, Ben Hogan, and a downhill putt."

—Sam Snead

◆

"It's like playing in a straitjacket. They just lay you up on the rack and twist on both ends."

—Ben Crenshaw, on the U.S. Open

"I shot a wild elephant in Africa thirty yards
from me, and it didn't hit the ground
until it was right at my feet. I wasn't a bit scared.
But a four-foot putt scares me to death."

—Sam Snead

◆

"You don't realize the pressure you're under
trying to make the cut. By Sunday you feel as if
you were in a prize fight."

—Dave Stockton

"Too many people carry the last shot with them.
It is a heavy and useless burden."

_Johnny Miller

◆

"Good golfing temperament falls between taking
it with a grin or shrug and throwing a fit."

_Sam Snead

◆

"I told him to hit it and run backwards."

_Ken Venturi, recounting the advice he gave a duffer who
wanted more distance on his tee shots

"Golf cannot be played in anger, or in any mood of emotional excess. Half the golf balls struck by amateurs are hit, if not in rage, surely in bewilderment, or gloom, or cynicism, or even hysterically—all of those emotional excesses which must be contained by a professional."

—Writer George Plimpton

"If a man can take five or six bogeys in a row, or a succession of flubbed shots without blowing his stack, he is capable of handling any situation."

—Jimmy Demaret

◆

"Good players have the power to think while they are competing. Most golfers are not thinking even when they believe they are. They are only worrying."

—Golf guru Harvey Penick

"Any time you save par out of the rough in this tournament, you feel like you've escaped from jail. It's like a get-out-of-jail-free card."

_Tom Lehman, on the U.S. Open

◆

"In other games you get another chance. In baseball you get three cracks at it; in tennis you lose only one point. But in golf the loss of one shot has been responsible for the loss of heart."

_Tommy Armour

"Golf is a game that creates emotions that sometimes cannot be sustained with the club still in one hand."

Bobby Jones

◆

"To succeed at anything, you must have a huge ego. I'm not talking about confidence. Confidence is self-assurance for a reason. Ego is self-assurance for no good reason."

Frank Beard

◆

"We really have to play with 15 clubs. The 14 in our bag and the 15th in our head."

Greg Twiggs

"The sport isn't like any other where a player can take out all that is eating him on an opponent. In golf, it's strictly you against your clubs."

Bob Rosburg

◆

"If you have to remind yourself to concentrate during competition, you've got no chance to concentrate."

Bobby Nichols

◆

"A lot of guys who have never choked have never been in the position to do so."

Tom Watson

"We all say majors are just another
72-hole tournament. In a way, they are.
But we're really just saying that to keep
ourselves from getting too fired up."

—Curtis Strange

"Jimmy Demaret and I had the best sports
psychologist in the world. His name was
Jack Daniels and he was waiting for us
after every round."

*—Former pro golfer Jackie Burke, criticizing modern players
for relying on so-called mental coaches*

"Unless you're able to comprehend the pressures of working for your paycheck each week, I don't know if you can have a true appreciation of the game. You can love it, you can be addicted to it, but I don't know if you appreciate how difficult it is . . . and how you can go from the top of the mountain to flat on your face."

ESPN broadcaster Dan Patrick

◆

"Golf inflicts more pain than any other sport. If you're the sort of person whose self-worth is tied up in how you play, golf will cut you to the core of who you are."

Sports psychologist James E. Loehr

"Every time I'd get close to a major prize, my hands would begin to shake, and for a moment or two, when it counted most, the demons of doubt would whisper in my ear and I honestly wondered if I could win again."

_Arnold Palmer, on the decline of his game

◆

"A golfer chokes when he lets anger, doubt, fear, or some other extraneous factor distract him before a shot."

_Dr. Bob Rotella, in GOLF IS NOT A GAME

"I will do everything I can to beat my opponents before the 18th hole."

—Ryder Cup candidate Jean Van de Velde, after self-destructing on the final hole of the 1999 British Open

"I had always suspected that trying to play golf in the company of big-time pros and a gallery would be something like walking naked into choir practice."

—Writer Dan Jenkins

"Golf is the only sport I know of where a player pays for every mistake. A man can muff a serve in tennis, miss a strike in baseball, or throw an incomplete pass in football and still have another chance to square himself. In golf, every swing counts against you."

—Lloyd Mangrum

◆

"There's going to come at least one point when you want to throw yourself in the nearest trash can and disappear. You know you can't hide. It's like walking down the fairway naked. The gallery knows what you've done, every other player knows, and worst of all, you know."

—Hale Irwin

"I would rather play Hamlet with no rehearsal than play golf on television."

—Actor Jack Lemmon

◆

"When I first came on tour, it terrified me to hit the first drive. I was lucky if I kept it in play. That feeling has disappeared for the most part, but I still feel it once in a while."

—Lon Hinkle

◆

"I go to the first tee scared to death every day. The peaks do not seem to last as long as the valleys in this game."

—J. C. Snead

"It takes years to build up your confidence, but it hardly takes a moment to lose it. Confidence is when you stand over a shot and know you're going to make it because you've done it time and time again."

—Jack Nicklaus

◆

"I have seen men who have won a dozen or more tournaments, upon teeing off for their first USGA Open Championship, come close to vomiting. And golf is no easy game when you are trying to hole a downhill three-footer and throwing up at the same time."

—Golf writer Charles Price

"When you are young and facing a 50-to-one shot through an opening in trees with a two-iron you say, 'What the heck?' and try it. You are so gifted physically and so ungifted mentally."

—Ray Floyd

◆

"All golfers fear the one-iron. It has no angle, no loft. The one-iron is a confidence-crusher, a fear trip, an almost guarantee of shame, failure, dumbness, and humiliation if you ever use it in public."

—Gonzo journalist Hunter S. Thompson

"By the time I got to the first tee in my first Masters, I was so scared I could hardly breathe. If you're not a little nervous there, there isn't anything in life that can make you nervous."

—Roger Maltbie

◆

"Basically, it's the inability to make your hands obey the commands your mind gives them."

—Johnny Miller, on the infamous "yips"

◆

"Golf is a game of the head as well as a game of the hands."

—U.S. Amateur champion Jerome Travers

"Golf is a game of inches. The most important are those between the ears."

—Arnold Palmer

"Let's face it, 95 percent of this game is mental. A guy plays lousy golf, he doesn't need a pro— he needs a shrink."

—Tom Murphy

"I say this without any reservations whatsoever: It is impossible to outplay an opponent you can't outthink."

—Lawson Little

"You start to choke at the Masters when you drive through the front gate."

—Hale Irwin

"Absolutely everyone has done it, but there are few people who admit it."

—David Feherty, on choking

Par for the Course

"According to the captain of the honourable Company of Edinburgh Golfers, striking your opponent or caddie at St. Andrews, Hoylake, or Westward Ho meant that you lost the hole, except on medal days when it counted as a rub of the green."

—Writer Herbert Warren Wind

◆

"A golf course is the epitome of all that is purely transitory in the universe—a space not to dwell in, but to get over as quickly as possible."

—French writer Jean Giraudoux

"Putting on Winged Foot greens is like playing miniature golf without the boards."

—Hale Irwin

◆

"This is the origin of the game, golf in its purest form; and it's still played that way on a course seemingly untouched by time. Every time I play here, it reminds me that this is still a game."

—Arnold Palmer, on the Old Course at St. Andrews

"I catch fish in water that is more shallow than the rough here."

_Phil Blackmar, casting aspersions on the Winged Foot golf course

◆

"We're not trying to humiliate the worst players in the world . . . we're trying to identify them."

_USGA president Frank Tatum, on the selection of tough U.S. Open courses

◆

"Columbus went around the world in 1492. That isn't a lot of strokes when you consider the course."

_Lee Trevino

"While man's battle against himself is undoubtedly at the heart of golf's abiding appeal, the setting in which it is played is, for most golfers, one of the most wonderful things about it."

Writer Herbert Warren Wind

◆

"There is absolutely nothing humorous at the Masters. Here, small dogs do not bark and babies do not cry."

Gary Player

"Every hole should be a hard par
and an easy bogey."

_Course designer Robert Trent Jones

◆

"They were rolling the carpets up behind us
the whole back nine."

_Ken Peyre-Ferry, after completing a round
at the 1998 U.S. Open at 8:54 P.M.

◆

"The scores have been lower than
Gary McCord's IQ."

_CBS golf analyst David Feherty, on the quality
of play during the 2001 golf season

"The worst piece of mess I've ever played. I think they had some sheep and goats there that died and they just covered them up."

—Scott Hoch, after playing Scotland's romanticized Old Course at St. Andrews

"To find a links course this good in the heartland of America is like swimming onto a deserted island and finding Ginger and Mary Ann cooking breakfast."

—Golf writer John Hawkins, on the Whistling Straights course that hugs Lake Michigan

◆

"I've never been to Heaven, and thinkin' back on my life, I probably won't get a chance to go. I guess the Masters is as close as I am going to get."

—Fuzzy Zoeller

"A golf course is an outdoor insane asylum peopled with madmen suffering from the delusion that they will finally master the game."

—Humorist Robert H. Davis

◆

"Putting the greens at Oakmont is like putting down a marble staircase and trying to stop the ball on the third step from the bottom."

—1936 U.S. Open champion Tony Manero

◆

"There's nothing wrong with the Old Course at St. Andrews that a hundred bulldozers couldn't put right."

—Ed Furgol

"Just because you cut the grass and put up flags doesn't mean you have a golf course. What this place lacks is 80 acres of corn and a few cows. The man who designed this golf course had his blueprints upside down."

_Dave Hill, on the Hazeltine course at the 1970 U.S. Open

◆

"Merion is like your grandmother: ancient, beautiful, to be loved and respected. But if you make one mistake, she'll whup you."

_The advice Ben Crenshaw received from his father before the 1971 U.S. Open

"Water holes are sacrificial waters where you make a steady gift of your pride and high-priced golf balls."

_Tommy Bolt

◆

"A good swamp spoiled."

_Gary Player, on the Carnoustie golf course

◆

"I don't think there's any way to Tiger-proof any golf course these days, short of pulling out the flagsticks."

_Keith Reese, Valhalla Golf Course head pro

"It's the only golf course I know of where you could have a 10-shot lead with two holes to play and have a good chance to blow it."

_Bruce Devlin, on the Tournament Players Club at Sawgrass

◆

"We could make the greens so slick we'd have to furnish ice skates on the first tee."

_Masters chairman Hord Hardin

◆

"We don't want heads to roll . . . we want greens to roll."

_Nick Faldo, protesting the poor conditions on the European Tour

"It's the only pure golf tournament we play in, including all of the other major championships. No skyboxes here or anything like that. You see the same faces in the gallery come tournament time. Over the years, I get to know the people and where they sit."

_Greg Norman, on the Masters

◆

"At St. Andrews you can hit pretty good shots and get shafted because the fairways are hard. The ball keeps rolling and ends up in a fairway bunker. You can also hit bad shots and finish perfect."

_Scott Hoch

"I consider it only fair to permit a golfer to get warmed to his game. If he does get into difficulties at the first couple of holes, it will materially affect his whole game and deteriorate his play; if he gets a good start, he is not only less likely to break down under the strain of difficult golf, but even if he does come to grief, it will not have the same depressing effect on his after play."

_Course designer Willie Park

◆

"Oakmont has the only church pews on earth where you go to cuss. Prayer won't help."

_Frank Nobilo, on the famous green-striped bunkers at Oakmont Country Club

"I lost a ball in your rough today. I dropped another ball over my shoulder and lost it too—and while looking for that one, I lost a caddie."

—Jock Hutchinson, complaining to an official about course conditions at the 1926 U.S. Open

◆

"If you can see the Mourne Mountains, it's going to rain; if you can't see them, it's raining."

—Forecast at the Royal County Down course in Newcastle, Northern Ireland

"The object of a bunker or trap is not only to punish a physical mistake—to punish a lack of control—but also to punish pride and egotism."

Course architect Charles Blair McDonald

◆

"There is no denying that golf has put Hilton Head on the map. After all, how many homes can you build around a tennis court?"

Golf writer Charles Price

"Golf should be a fair test. If the average golfer shoots 90, he'll be comfortable. If he shoots 120, he'll want to give up the game."

_Course designer Robert Trent Jones

◆

"Game plan? St. Andrews is the only course in the world where the only thing you try to do is miss all the bunkers. That's the game plan."

_Steve Elkington

"You're like a blind man with a pretty girl—
you have to feel your way around."

Peter Jacobsen, on the Royal St. George course

"In Britain, you skip the ball, hop it, bump it,
run it, hit under it, on top of it, and then hope
for the right bounce."

Doug Sanders

"Golf wasn't meant to be fair."

Golf course architect Pete Dye

◆

"If you try to fight the course, it will beat you."

Lou Graham

Amateur Hour

"The things I have seen in the Ryder Cup have disappointed me. You are hearing about hatred and war."

—Gary Player

◆

"Golf is the only game where the worst player gets the best of it. He gets more out of it with regard to both exercise and enjoyment. The good player worries over the slightest mistake, whereas the poor player makes too many mistakes to worry over them."

—British Prime Minister David Lloyd George

"Golf is so popular because it is the best game in the world at which to be bad . . . At golf, it is the bad player who gets the most strokes."

—*Author A. A. Milne*

◆

"I was three over—one over a house, one over a patio, and one over a swimming pool."

—*Baseball Hall of Famer George Brett, on his golf game*

◆

"I'm one under. One under a tree, one under a rock, one under a bush . . ."

—*Pro hockey goalie Gary Cheevers, on his golf game*

"Lots of golfers spend their time wondering whether to lay up or go for it. I'm always going for it because that's the way I play football."

—Green Bay Packers quarterback Brett Favre

◆

"If you drink, don't drive. Don't even putt."

—Entertainer Dean Martin

◆

"Mulligan: invented by an Irishman who wanted to hit one more 20-yard grounder."

—Columnist Jim Bishop

"My best score is 103. But I've
only been playing 15 years."

_Pro football player Alex Karras

◆

"Pick up the ball, have the clubs destroyed,
and leave the course."

_British journalist Viscount Castlerosse, to his caddie
after topping three straight balls

◆

"A golfer is someone with
hoof and mouth disease. He hoofs it all day
and mouths it all night."

_Humorist Will Rogers

"I tried everything mental and physical I could to help him out. After three or four holes, there was nothing I could do. I ran out of ideas. I just told him, 'I feel for you. I really do.'"

—Tom Watson, after being paired with NBA all-star Charles Barkley at a pro-am

◆

"I'm going to give you my secret of golf. You can't play a really great game unless you're so miserable that you don't worry over your shots . . . Look at the top-notchers. Come on, have you ever seen a happy pro?"

—Humorist P. G. Wodehouse

"When golf season comes around, I get like a piano player who doesn't shake hands with anybody for fear of hurting himself. What if I'm weight lifting and I drop a weight on my hands? What if I throw my shoulder out? Then I would be miserable. Just absolutely miserable. I haven't reached an accommodation with that phobia, so here I sit, fat and soft."

_TV personality Bryant Gumbel

"You've just got one problem. You stand too close to the ball after you've hit it."

—Sam Snead, to a duffer

◆

"After an abominable round of golf, a man is known to have slit his wrists with a razor blade and, having bandaged them, to have stumbled into the locker room and inquired of his partner, 'What time tomorrow?'"

—British journalist Alistair Cooke

"I've lost balls in every hazard and on every course I've tried. But when I lose a ball in the ball washer, it's time to take stock."

—Author Milton Gross

◆

"I just can't find it when I hit it."

—NBA Hall of Famer Jerry West, on his golf game

◆

"The pleasure I get from hitting the ball dead center on the club is comparable only to one or two other pleasures that come to mind at the moment."

—Entertainer and golf lover Dinah Shore

"Give me my golf clubs, the fresh air, and a beautiful partner, and you can keep my golf clubs and the fresh air."

Comedian Bob Hope

"Thinking you are going to win the Crosby Pro-Am with a high handicap makes as much sense as leaving the porch light on for Jimmy Hoffa."

Bill Harris

"If you think it's hard to meet new people, try picking up the wrong golf ball."

Actor Jack Lemmon

"It matters not the sacrifice which makes the duffer's wife so sore. I am the captive of my slice, I am the servant of my score."

—Sportswriter Grantland Rice

◆

"I play in the low 80s. If it's any hotter than that, I won't play."

—Boxing great Joe Louis

◆

"A professional will tell you the amount of flex you need in the shaft of your club. The more the flex, the more strength you will need to break the thing over your knee."

—Writer Stephen Baker

"The hardest shot is a mashie at 90 yards from the green, where the ball has to be played against an oak tree, bounces back into a sand trap, hits a stone, bounces on the green, and then rolls into the cup. The shot is so difficult I have only made it once."

Comedian Zeppo Marx

◆

"How do I address the ball? I say, 'Hello there, ball. Are you going to go in the hole or not?'"

Comedian Flip Wilson

"I never pray on the golf course. Actually, the Lord answers my prayers everywhere except on the course."

_The Reverend Billy Graham

◆

"On the practice range, he drives it to places that make your head spin. After he got warmed up and got a sweat going, he started hitting balls over the fence at the end of the range. Everyone oohed and aahed."

_Billy Andrade, on golf buddy and baseball slugger Mark McGwire

"Baffling late-life discovery:
Golfers wear those awful clothes on purpose."

Columnist Herb Caen

◆

"We believe you can enjoy the great game of golf
without taking it so seriously. No lying, no
cheating, and no sandbagging necessary
because your golf score, fact or fiction,
doesn't mean a flip."

_Max Colclasure, founder of the
Laid Back Golfers Association_

"I beat Tiger Woods by five strokes—
but he was only six at the time."

_Kansas City Royals catcher Gregg Zaun, on competing
against wunderkind Woods as a junior

◆

"Probably I'm a hell of a lot more famous for
being the guy who hit the golf ball on the moon
than the first guy in space."

_Apollo 14 astronaut Alan Shepard

"Once when I was golfing in Georgia, I hooked the ball into the swamp. I went in after it and found an alligator wearing a shirt with a picture of a little golfer on it."

—Comedian Buddy Hackett

◆

"As long as they don't call me 'Old Lady Thompson,' I think it's great."

—Veteran amateur Carol Semple Thompson, on the new wave of young players competing at the 1999 U.S. Women's Amateur

"I'll take a two-stroke penalty. But I'll be damned if I'll play it where it lies."

_Elaine Johnson, after her mishit ball landed inside her bra

◆

"There are no bad calls."

_Tennis star Ivan Lendl, on why he likes golf

Swing Thoughts

"I think they should ban all drivers.
Just use irons."

_Two-time Masters champion Jose Maria Olazabal,
one of the wildest drivers in professional golf

◆

"The only natural golfer is a kid at five years old.
Everyone else has to adjust their swings.
Otherwise, we would go to the moon on a
catapult if we didn't make any changes."

_Nick Faldo

"The follow-through is that part of the golf swing
that takes place after the ball has been struck,
but before the club has been thrown."

—Humorist Henry Beard

◆

"Don't change the arc of your swing unless
you are fairly sure you blundered
in some way earlier."

—Sportswriter Rex Lardner

"To get an elementary grasp of the game of golf, a human must learn, by endless practice, a continuous and subtle series of highly unnatural movements, involving about 64 muscles, that result in a seemingly natural swing, taking all of two seconds to begin and end."

_British journalist Alistair Cooke

◆

"After taking the stance, it is too late to worry. The only thing to do then is to hit the ball."

_Bobby Jones

"Hitting a golf ball correctly is the most sophisticated and complicated maneuver in all of sports, with the possible exception of eating a hot dog at a ball game without getting mustard on your shirt."

—Sportswriter Ray Fitzgerald

◆

"He took a swing like a man with a wasp under his shorts and his pants on fire, trying to impale a butterfly on the end of a scythe."

—Sportswriter Paul Gallico, describing his playing partner

"When you lose your swing, you might just as well quit walking around in the sun and get in the shade."

—Jimmy Demaret

◆

"If you think your hands are more important in your golf swing than your legs, try walking a hole on your hands."

—Gary Player

◆

"When I'm swinging bad, I need to go to the range. When I'm swinging good, I go to the Cabernet."

—Mark Wiebe

"The Golf Hall of Fame is full of players with unusual-looking swings. Some of the prettiest swings you've ever seen in your life are made on the far end of the public driving range by guys who couldn't break an egg with a baseball bat."

—Peter Jacobsen

◆

"My swing works for me, so why should I change it? I prefer to have a natural swing and play well rather than a perfect swing and not be able to play good."

—Sergio Garcia, answering critics of his swing

"My God, he looks like he's beating a chicken!"

—Byron Nelson, on actor Jack Lemmon's swing

"The golf swing is like sex. You can't be thinking about the mechanics of the act while you are performing."

_Dave Hill

"I'm finding out that I just don't have as good a swing as I thought I had."

_Amateur Jim Holtgrieve, after joining the pro Senior Tour

The Game of Golf

"Miss Manners is shocked to learn that golfers are yelling anything other than 'Fore!' on the golf course, or striking anything other than golf balls with their clubs. Golf is the very last sport Miss Manners would expect to require an umpire, and she hopes everyone out on the fairways will get a grip on their civility before it comes to that."

—Miss Manners (Judith Martin)

◆

"The first chapter in the *Rules of Golf* is etiquette. Apparently everyone starts reading at chapter two."

—Cog Hill general manager Nick Mokelke

"Beyond the fact that it is a limitless arena for the full play of human nature, there is no sure accounting for golf's fascination. . . . Perhaps it is nothing more than the best game man has ever devised."

—Golf writer Herbert Warren Wind

◆

"It takes six years to make a golfer: three to learn the game, then another three to unlearn all you have learned in the first three years. You might be a golfer when you arrive at that stage, but more likely you are just starting."

—Walter Hagen

"It is almost impossible to remember how tragic
a place the world is when one is playing golf."

—Sociologist Robert Lynd

◆

"Every golfer has a little monster in him.
It's just that type of sport."

—Fuzzy Zoeller

◆

"Golf and women are a lot alike. You know you
are not going to wind up with anything but grief,
but you can't resist the impulse."

—Comedian Jackie Gleason

"Here's the ball and there's the hole, four and a quarter inches in diameter. We're expected to get the ball from here to there in three shots, across all this land and water. And what's more amazing, sometimes we do it in one shot. It boggles the mind to even think of it."

Pro golfer Dan Halldorson

◆

"A golf ball simply cannot find the hole by itself. Even if it could, the ball would never do so willingly, after the hatred and hammering you've heaped on it to get it to the green."

Cartoonist Dick Brooks

"One of the most fascinating things about golf is how it reflects the cycle of life. No matter what you shoot, the next day you have to go back to the first tee and begin all over again and make yourself into something."

—Peter Jacobsen

◆

"On the golf course, a man may be the dogged victim of inexorable fate, be struck down by an appalling stroke of tragedy, become the hero of unbelievable melodrama, or the clown in a side-splitting comedy."

—Bobby Jones

"Golf is the hardest game in the world. There's no way you can ever get it. Just when you think you do, the game jumps up and puts you in your place."

_Ben Crenshaw

◆

"I couldn't keep them lit."

_Senior PGA Tour player Roger Maltbie, explaining why his attempt to quit smoking using nicotine patches failed

◆

"In case you don't know very much about the game of golf, a good one-iron shot is about as easy to come by as an understanding wife."

_Writer Dan Jenkins

"Like one's own children, golf has an uncanny way of endearing itself to us while at the same time evoking every weakness of mind and character, no matter how well hidden."

—*Sportswriter W. Timothy Gallwey*

◆

"Just when you think you've got the game conquered, the game conquers you."

—*Michael Jordan, after shooting rounds of 84 and 81 at the 1999 Chicago Open*

"Unlike the other Scotch game of whisky-drinking, excess is not injurious to the health."

—Nineteenth-century golf writer Sir Walter Simpson, on the growing popularity of golf in 1879

◆

"In golf, when we hit a foul ball, we got to go out and play it."

—Sam Snead to Baseball Hall of Famer Ted Williams

◆

"There is no better game in the world when you are in good company, and no worse game when you are in bad company."

—Tommy Bolt

"As every golfer knows, no one ever lost his mind over one shot. It is rather the gradual process of shot after shot watching your score go to tatters . . . knowing that you have found a different way to bogey each one."

Sportswriter Thomas Boswell

"It is the constant and undying hope for improvement that makes golf so exquisitely worth playing."

Golf writer Bernard Darwin

"Golf puts a man's character on the anvil and his richest qualities—patience, poise, restraint— to the flame."

Billy Casper

◆

"Golf gives you an insight into human nature, your own as well as your opponent's. Eighteen holes of match or medal play will teach you more about your foe than will 18 years of dealing with him across a desk."

Sportswriter Grantland Rice

"While playing golf, your partners give you praise and encouragement even when you are not performing well. I don't remember this ever happening in the bedroom."

—A reader answering an Ann Landers "Golf versus Sex" survey

◆

"Golfers make better lovers because they have such great touch. In golf you have to be good in all areas. You have to be powerful, be strong, have stamina, and be able to control yourself. All those things are important in making love."

—Jan Stephenson

"Golf is assuredly a mystifying game.
It would seem that if a person has hit a golf ball
correctly a thousand times, he should be able to
duplicate the performance at will. But such
is certainly not the case."

—Bobby Jones

◆

"Golf is assuredly a mystifying game.
Even the best golfers cannot step onto the first
tee with any assurance as to what they
are going to do."

—Sportswriter W. Timothy Gallwey